An
American Girl's

Family Album

A Book for Writing the Memories of
My Grandmothers, My Mother, and Me

PLEASANT COMPANY

Published by Pleasant Company Publications
© Copyright 1998 by Pleasant Company
All rights reserved. No part of this book may be used or reproduced
in any manner whatsoever without written permission except in
the case of brief quotations embodied in critical articles and reviews.
For information, address: Book Editor, Pleasant Company Publications,
8400 Fairway Place, P.O. Box 620998, Middleton, WI 53562.

Printed in the United States of America.
99 00 01 02 03 04 WCV 10 9 8 7 6 5 4 3 2

Felicity®, Felicity Merriman®, Josefina®, Josefina Montoya®, Kirsten®,
Kirsten Larson®, Addy®, Addy Walker®, Molly®, Molly McIntire®,
and The American Girls Collection® are trademarks of Pleasant Company.

Written by Jennifer Hirsch and Jeanne Thieme
Illustrated by D.J. Simison, Dan Andreasen, Nick Backes, Renée Graef, Dahl Taylor, and Jean-Paul Tibbles
Edited by Jennifer Hirsch
Designed and Art Directed by Pat Tuchscherer and Jane Varda
Produced by Mary Cudnohfsky and Cheryll Mellenthin

I Remember . . .

*I*t's easy to remember some things, like your name, what you did yesterday, and how you celebrated your last birthday. But other things are easy to forget. Do you remember the first word you said? Can you still tell the story of your first day at school?

Stories about things that happened in the past are *history*. History books tell stories about events like wars and new discoveries that changed people's lives. They tell stories about important people like George Washington, Susan B. Anthony, and Martin Luther King Jr. History books also tell stories about everyday people and how they lived.

You can write a history book because you have a history. By remembering, and writing down what you remember, you will begin to tell the story of your life—and to write your own history.

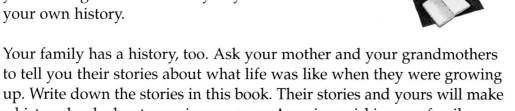

Your family has a history, too. Ask your mother and your grandmothers to tell you their stories about what life was like when they were growing up. Write down the stories in this book. Their stories and yours will make a history book about growing up as an American girl in your family. Your history book will show how some things have changed for girls in America, while other things haven't changed at all.

Written memories are called *memoirs* (pronounced MEM-wahrz— the second syllable rhymes with "cars"). Memoirs are a wonderful way to tell the story of your life and your family because you—and other people—can read them in the future to learn about life in the past. Historians even use people's memoirs to study history!

*T*ry to find a quiet time to write down your memories and to talk with your mother and grandmothers about theirs. Fill in your **Family Album** as you talk, or take notes during your talk and write the stories in this book later. If you can't visit, use the telephone or send letters or e-mail. (Just be sure to get permission before you make long-distance calls.)

If your mother or a grandmother is not available, ask other relatives to tell you stories about that person's life. Or you might choose to tell the story of a different relative who is like a mother or a grandmother to you, such as your stepmother or a great-aunt.

1

Felicity • 1774

Felicity Merriman lived in the Virginia colony at the start of the Revolutionary War. Her family believed that America should be its own country instead of an English colony.

Josefina • 1824

Josefina Montoya lived in colonial New Mexico at a time when America was growing rapidly. As more Americans came west, they brought new goods and new ways of life to Josefina's family.

Kirsten • 1854

Kirsten Larson and her family moved from Sweden to America to become pioneers. The Larsons faced hardships but also celebrated happy times on the Minnesota prairie.

Every Family Has a Story

Felicity Merriman, Josefina Montoya, Kirsten Larson, Addy Walker, Samantha Parkington, and Molly McIntire are six imaginary American girls from long ago. The American Girls and their stories can help you think about your own story—and your history.

Felicity was growing up when America was just becoming a country. Do you have ancestors who lived in America as far back as Felicity's time, at the beginning of our nation?

Life for Josefina changed in many ways as America's frontier moved west. Find out how changes in America affected the lives of your mother and grandmother when they were growing up.

Kirsten became an American girl when her family *immigrated,* or moved, to America from Sweden. Is there an immigration story in your family history? If you don't know, ask your grandmothers to tell you where *their* parents and grandparents came from.

Addy's family moved from the South to the North, from the country to the city, from slavery to freedom. Has your family made any big moves in the past? Or experienced big changes in the way they lived?

Samantha didn't have a mother who could tell her stories about growing up in another time. But other people remembered Samantha's mother, and the stories they told became part of Samantha's story and the story of her family. Your aunts, uncles, and grandfathers can tell you more about your mother and grandmothers when they were girls.

Molly grew up when your grandmothers might have been young girls. Ask your grandmothers to tell you about what they did on the home front during World War Two. You might be surprised by their schemes and dreams!

You probably won't write your whole family history in one afternoon. It takes time to remember—and to write—good stories. The story-starters in this book will help you begin. Use them to ask questions about what it was like to grow up in other times. Going through old letters and photographs is another way to spark memories and family stories.

When you finish this book, save it. Someday, you may want to share your *Family Album* with your own American girl! For her, the story of your life today will be a story about growing up in times past. It will be as interesting to her as your mother's and grandmothers' stories are to you.

Addy • 1864

Addy Walker and her family made a courageous flight to freedom while America was fighting the Civil War to end slavery. Addy began her new life in Philadelphia as a free American.

Samantha • 1904

Samantha Parkington was an orphan being raised by her wealthy grandmother at the turn of the century, a time of far-reaching changes, new inventions, and new ideas in America.

Molly • 1944

Molly McIntire was growing up on the home front during World War Two. The McIntires coped with shortages of food and goods, and worried about Molly's father, who was a doctor in the war.

Family Names

*Family names can sometimes give you clues about where your ancestors used to live and what they used to do. Molly McIntire's ancestors came from Scotland. Names that begin with **Mc** or **Mac** are usually Scottish or Irish. In the language spoken in Scotland and Ireland long ago, Mc and Mac meant "son of."*

*Kirsten's family got a new name in 1854 when they left the ship that brought them to America. In Sweden, Kirsten's last name was Lars**dotter** because Papa's name was Lars and she was his daughter. Kirsten's brother was named Peter Lar**son** because he was the son of Lars. Kirsten's family wanted to be like other Americans, so in America, they all called themselves the Larsons. (Papa's father was named Lars, too!)*

Your family name is your last name, or your *surname*. In the past, most American women took their husbands' family names when they married. Today, some women keep their original family names when they marry.

Babies are sometimes named for other people in their families. A girl might be named for her mother or grandmother. A boy might be named for his father or grandfather. Were you named for anyone in your family?

A family tree is a place to record the names of your ancestors. Fill in their names on the branches of the tree at right:

1. Start with yourself. Write your full name at the bottom of the tree.

2. Add your parents' full names on the first two branches. Your mother's branch is the *maternal* branch of your family tree. *Mater* is the Latin word for "mother." Your father's branch is the *paternal* branch of your family tree. *Pater* is the Latin word for "father."

3. Next add your grandparents' full names. Your maternal grandparents are your mother's parents. Your paternal grandparents are your father's parents.

4. Ask your parents and grandparents to help you add your great-grandparents' names. Your maternal great-grandparents are your mother's grandparents. Your paternal great-grandparents are your father's grandparents.

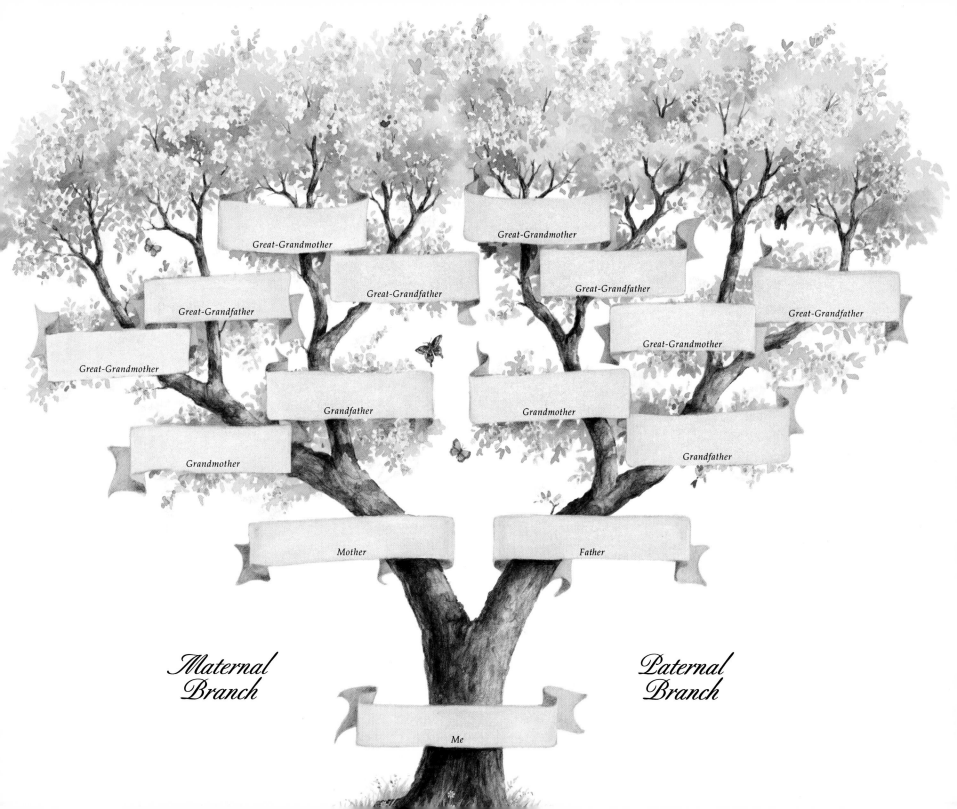

Great-Grandmother

Great-Grandmother

Great-Grandfather

Great-Grandfather

Great-Grandfather

Great-Grandmother

Great-Grandfather

Great-Grandmother

Grandfather

Grandmother

Grandmother

Grandfather

Mother

Father

Maternal Branch

Paternal Branch

Me

My Ancestors

People in my mother's family who came to America from other countries:

Name   *Old Country*   *When Ancestor Came to America*

....

....

....

People in my father's family who came to America from other countries:

Name   *Old Country*   *When Ancestor Came to America*

....

....

....

Before my family spoke English, we spoke ....

                                                                list languages

I can say some things in my ancestors' languages:

Name of Language   *What I Can Say*   *English Meaning*

....

....

....

....

Nearly every American girl today has one or more ancestors who came to America from another country. Your parents, grandparents, great-grandparents, and all their relatives who came before them are your ancestors. Use a globe or a map to find the "old country" where your ancestors used to live. How long ago did they come to America?

In their old countries, your ancestors probably had different jobs, customs, and clothing from those your family has today. They may have eaten different kinds of food and lived in different kinds of housing. See what you can find out about your ancestors' ways of life in the old country.

My mother's ancestors lived in ....
                                        name of town or city, country

where they worked as ....
                                        jobs they had

My father's ancestors lived in ....
                                        name of town or city, country

where they worked as ....
                                        jobs they had

An interesting job one of my ancestors had was ....

My ancestors celebrated holidays such as ....

Some of their customs were ....
                                Describe special clothing, songs, traditions, daily habits, or beliefs.

....

A food my ancestors ate that seems strange to me today is ....

Foods my ancestors ate that we still eat today include ....

                        We eat them ....
                                                when

Some of my ancestors kept animals such as ....

They used the animals for ....

When they came to America, my ancestors traveled by ....

They brought with them ....

They left behind ....

*Josefina's ancestors came from Spain. They would have arrived in the New World, or America, in the 1500s. They traveled in great sailing ships called **galleons**. They knew they would probably never return to Spain, so they brought their families. Livestock such as horses, sheep, and chickens also came on the galleons. Along with their Catholic faith, the Spaniards brought stories, songs, dances, and holiday traditions from Spain—and they kept the same language, Spanish.*

My Story

My full name is ....

but some people call me ....

I was given my name because ....

....

I am .... years old. I was born at .... in ....
time and date *hospital or place, city, state*

.... I weighed .... pounds and was .... inches long.

People said that I looked ....

Today I live with ....
names of family members

....

We have a pet .... named ....

Other pets include ....

Our address is ....

From the outside, my home looks ....

....

My favorite place is ....

because ....

....

Some of my jobs at home are ....

*T*he word **felicity** means
"happiness." Grandfather
told Felicity, "With your birth
began a joy unlike any other
we'd ever known." Perhaps
that's why her parents chose
the name. Colonists sometimes
named their children after
virtues, such as Patience,
Constance, Prudence, or
Charity. Felicity even named
her horse after a virtue—
Independence, or Penny
for short.

My mother works

My father works

My family has fun by

My best friends are named

When we are together, we

Our favorite thing to do together is

I like my friends because

They like me because

I am proud of myself for

I am still embarrassed about the time I

My favorite things and activities are

When I grow up, I want to

Before I go to sleep at night, I think about

Kirsten had lots of pets—
Caro the dog, Missy the
cat and her kittens, and even
a baby raccoon! On a frontier
farm, pets had jobs just as
people did. And pets lived
where they worked. Cats lived
in the barn, where they caught
mice. Dogs lived outside,
where they guarded pioneers
from danger. Wild animals like
raccoons were not good pets.
They belonged in the woods!

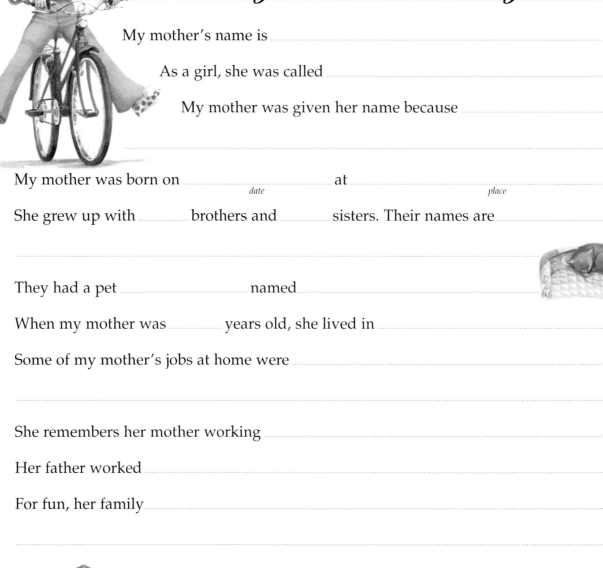

My Mother's Story

My mother's name is ....

As a girl, she was called ....

My mother was given her name because ....

....

My mother was born on .... at ....
                              date   *place*

She grew up with .... brothers and .... sisters. Their names are .....

....

They had a pet .... named ....

When my mother was .... years old, she lived in ....

Some of my mother's jobs at home were ....

....

She remembers her mother working ....

Her father worked ....

For fun, her family ....

....

As a girl, my mother enjoyed ....

....

In 1944, when Molly was growing up, America was fighting in World War Two. Many men went away to be soldiers or to work in the war, like Molly's dad. Before the war, most American women did not have jobs outside the home. But as men went away to fight, more and more women went to work in offices and factories. They proved that women can do any job that needs to be done.

People said she looked like

She wanted to be a .... when she grew up.

When she was .... years old, my mother's best friends were ....

.... Their favorite

activity to do together was ....

The worst thing my mother did when she was growing up was ....

....

She is still proud of the time that she ....

....

When she was a girl, my mother used to worry about ....

because ....

Her happiest times were when ....

....

My mother met my father in .... My mother was .... years old. My father was ....
              year

years old. They lived in ....
                                               place

Later, they moved to ....

My mother was .... years old when I was born. She thinks the best thing about being my

mother is ....

....

Mamá died when Josefina was eight years old. Cameras were not yet invented in 1824, so Josefina had no photographs of her mother. Instead, she kept her memories alive by collecting **mementos**, or small things that reminded her of Mamá—a piece of Mamá's lavender soap, a dried primrose, Mamá's silver thimble. She stored the precious mementos in her memory box.

My Grandmother's Story

My mother's mother is named ....

As a girl, she was called ....

My mother called her ....

Today, I call her ....

My mother's mother was born on .... at ....
                                   date   *place*

She had .... brothers and .... sisters named ....

....

Their pets were ....

They lived in ....
                      type of house or apartment, town or city, state

When she was growing up, some of my grandmother's jobs at home were ....

....

Her mother worked ....

Her father worked ....

For fun, her family used to ....

Her favorite activity was ....

Grandmother was married on .... She was .... years old. When my
                                   date

mother was born, Grandmother was .... years old. She thinks the best thing about being

a grandmother is ....

*A*ddy was named for her grandmother Aduke (ah-DOO-kay), which means "much loved" in Yoruba, an African language. People like Addy's grandmother were brought from Africa to America in trading ships to become slaves. Enslaved girls had to work hard at an early age. Later, in freedom, Addy still worked hard, but she was paid for her work.

My Grandmother's Story

My father's mother is named ....

As a girl, she was called ....

My father called her ....

Today, I call her ....

My father's mother was born on .... at ....
                                             date   place

She had .... brothers and .... sisters named ....

....

Their pets were ....

They lived in ....
                            type of house or apartment, town or city, state

When she was growing up, some of my grandmother's jobs at home were ....

....

Her mother worked ....

Her father worked ....

For fun, her family used to ....

Her favorite activity was ....

Grandmother was married on .... She was .... years old. When my
                                                date

father was born, Grandmother was .... years old. She thinks the best thing about being

a grandmother is ....

In Samantha's time, wealthy Victorian women like Grandmary believed that girls should have quiet, dignified activities, such as sewing a sampler, practicing the piano—and staying out of mischief! It was improper for a well-bred girl or woman to work, even in her own home. Samantha never had to set the table or make her bed. Servants did those jobs.

My School Story

I am in the _____ grade at _____
school

in _____ My school is _____
city, state how far

from my home. I get there by _____
bus, car, walking, bicycle

It takes _____ My school day starts at _____ A.M.
how long

and ends at _____ P.M. There are _____ students in my class.

My teacher's name is _____

I (like/don't like) my teacher because _____
circle one

_____

My favorite school subject is _____

I also like _____

I don't like _____ , because _____

_____

When I get good grades, _____

_____

If my grades are not good, _____

_____

In my school, we use _____ to help us learn.
tools, equipment

My own school supplies include _____

In Kirsten's school, children of all ages studied together in the same room. But they studied different lessons, depending on which grade they were in. Many days, bad weather or farm work kept pioneer children from going to school. So a girl like Kirsten might need three or four years to finish third grade. She didn't get a report card each year. Instead, when she learned a lesson well, the teacher gave her a Reward of Merit.

14

My school colors are

My best friends at school are

At recess, my friends and I

Lunchtime is at ____ o'clock. I eat
where

My favorite school lunch is

When I buy lunch at school, it costs ____ When I bring my lunch, I carry it in a

After school, I often

My favorite school project was

For a class trip, we

A special school activity this year is

I will go to school until I have finished

Then I plan to

The most important lesson I have learned in school is

Addy didn't start going to school until she was nine years old, but with her friend Sarah's help she caught up quickly. She even won the spelling match! Students in Addy's time had to study more than reading and math. Teachers like Miss Dunn taught them to be thrifty, orderly, and patriotic. And Addy learned something else, too—the value of a true friend like Sarah.

My Mother's School Story

My mother started school when she was .... years old. Her first school

was .... in ....
school name   *city, state*

Later, she went to ....
school names

When she was my age, my mother's school was ....
school name

in .... It was .... from home.
city, state   *how far*

She got there by .... It took ....
bus, car, walking, bicycle   *how long*

School started at .... A.M. and ended at .... P.M. There were .... students in her

class. The teacher's name was ....

My mother (liked/didn't like) this teacher because ....
circle one

Her best friends at school were ....

At recess they used to play ....

My mother ate lunch .... Her favorite school lunch
where

was .... She took .... to school to buy lunch.
how much money

For school supplies, my mother had ....

Her classrooms had equipment like ....

Her school clothes were ....

After school, my mother liked to ....

*I*n Samantha's time, physical education was important. Sports for girls included golf, lawn tennis, fencing, and gymnastics. Most public schools didn't have gym equipment, so students used their desks to practice gymnastics. They would balance on their desks or swing between them like parallel bars. Girls didn't have leotards—they wore their regular dresses!

16

My mother most enjoyed .... grade at .... School.

She liked it best because ....

....

My mother's favorite teacher was .... because

.... Her favorite subjects were ....

....

My mother didn't like .... because ....

....

A special school project or event she remembers is ....

....

When my mother brought home good grades, ...

.... If my mother's grades were not good, ...

....

My mother went to school until she was .... years old. Then she ....

....

If my mother could change one thing about her school days, she would ....

....

The most important lesson my mother learned in school is ....

....

Schools were rare in New Mexico in 1824. Like Josefina, most children were taught the skills they needed at home. Schools that did exist were very demanding. Class went from 6:00 A.M. to 5:00 P.M., six days a week. There was no recess, only a short break for breakfast and a longer one for lunch and siesta. Schools didn't have bells—instead, students looked at a sundial to tell time!

My Grandmother's School Story

My mother's mother started school when she was .... years old. When

she was my age, she went to ....
school name

....in ....
city, state

School was .... from her home. She got there by ....
how far   bus, car, walking, bicycle

It took .... There were .... students in her class.
how long

The teacher's name was .... My grandmother

(liked / didn't like) this teacher because ....
circle one

For school clothes, my grandmother wore ....

At recess, she played .... She ate lunch ....
where

Her favorite school lunch was ....

Her favorite teacher was ....

Her favorite school subjects were ....

My grandmother didn't like ....

because ....

A special school project or event was ....

My mother's mother went to school until she was .... years old. Then she ....

.... The most important lesson

my grandmother learned in school is ....

*M*usic was an important part of schooling in Felicity's time. But girls weren't allowed to play certain instruments. Since a girl was always supposed to have a pleasant expression on her face, it was improper for her to blow into a recorder or flute, or twist her neck to hold a violin! Instead, girls played harpsichords, which are similar to pianos, and guitars like the one Grandfather gave Felicity.

My Grandmother's School Story

My father's mother started school when she was .... years old. When

she was my age, she went to ....
school name

in ....
city, state

School was .... from her home. She got there by ....
how far   bus, car, walking, bicycle

It took .... There were .... students in her class.
how long

The teacher's name was .... My grandmother

(liked/didn't like) this teacher because ....
circle one

For school clothes, my grandmother wore ....

At recess, she played .... She ate lunch ....
where

Her favorite school lunch was ....

Her favorite teacher was ....

Her favorite school subjects were ....

My grandmother didn't like ....

because ....

A special school project or event was ....

My father's mother went to school until she was .... years old. Then she ....

.... The most important lesson

my grandmother learned in school is ....

During World War Two, children like Molly studied the war every day in school. They discussed what they had read in newspapers and heard on the radio. In geography, they studied maps showing where American troops were fighting. In art, they drew pictures of military planes. Trying to spot fighter planes was a favorite activity— but only Emily had seen real fighters flying overhead!

My Holiday Story

In 1904 it wasn't common—
or proper—for children to
buy the presents they gave,
even in a well-to-do household
like Samantha's. Instead,
children spent hours planning
and carefully making their
gifts, as Samantha did with
her scrap-paper box for Uncle
Gard and her heart sachet for
Grandmary. In Samantha's
time, handmade gifts were gifts
of love, just as they are today.

My family has a holiday celebration on ....
                                                        date

for ....
                                        name of holiday

We celebrate at ....
                                                        place

with ....
                            people who share your celebration

Our celebration begins with ....

Then we ....

Our celebration is over when ....

Our holiday foods are ....

....

My favorite food is ....

For holiday decorations, we ....

....

My favorite decoration is ....

For the holiday, I wear ....

Some things about our holiday are always the same. These are our traditions: ....

....

....

My favorite holiday tradition is ....

That tradition began when ....

....

Presents (are/are not) a big part of our holiday celebration. The best gift I ever
circle one

gave was .... , which I gave to ....

I chose that gift because ....

....

A gift I will never forget is ....

It was given to me by .... because ....

....

Something different that happened in our celebration this year was ....

....

....

....

.... I (do/don't) think this will become a new tradition in our family.
circle one

To me, the best thing about .... is ....
name of holiday

....

Other special holidays for my family are ....

I always hope that ....

*In Josefina's time, travel was slow and dangerous, so relatives who lived far away did not visit at Christmas. Instead, everyone in the village celebrated together. Each night for nine nights they walked together from house to house, singing and sharing the joy of **Las Posadas**, a reenactment of the story of Mary, Joseph, and baby Jesus. Josefina felt as if everyone she knew and loved were right there with her.*

My Mother's Holiday Story

As a girl, my mother celebrated ....
name of holiday

on .... She celebrated with ....
date *people who were there*

....

.... at ....
place

At their celebration, they ....

....

My mother's favorite holiday food was ....

Her family also ate ....

....

They decorated for the holiday with ....

....

My mother thought the most beautiful decoration was ....

Today, that decoration is ....
Tell who has the decoration and where it is used.

For the holiday, my mother wore ....

My mother's favorite holiday tradition was ....

....

Other holiday traditions in her family were ....

....

Kirsten's family and other Swedish immigrants brought their holiday traditions with them from Sweden to America. They started the Christmas season by celebrating St. Lucia's Day on December 13, bringing light and festivity to one of the darkest days of the year. Six months later they celebrated Midsummer on June 24 with picnics, music, and dancing.

Something she did that is still a tradition in my family is

Presents (were/were not) a big part of holiday celebrations when my mother was a girl. The

circle one

best gift my mother ever gave was

Tell what she gave, to whom she gave it, and when.

A gift she will never forget is

Tell what she received, who gave it, and when.

My mother and father spent their first holiday together at

A new tradition began when

The first time my mother celebrated

holiday

with me, she remembers

To my mother, the best thing about

holiday

is

Other special holidays in her family were

She always hopes that

F or Felicity, the holiday season lasted until January 6, or Twelfth Night, when the grandest parties were held. People didn't exchange presents at Christmas, but children and servants might receive small gifts on New Year's Day. Christmastide was joyful, but it meant a lot of extra cooking, cleaning, and sewing—and it was especially hard for Felicity when Mother became ill.

My Grandmother's Holiday Story

As a girl, my mother's mother celebrated ....

holiday

on .... My grandmother's favorite holiday food

date

was ....

Her family also ate ....

They decorated with ....

My grandmother thought the most beautiful decoration was ....

Today, that decoration is ....

Grandmother's favorite holiday clothes were ....

Her favorite tradition was ....

Something she did that is still a family tradition is ....

....

Presents (were/were not) a big part of holiday celebrations when my grandmother was a

circle one

girl because ....

A story my grandmother tells about .... when my mother

holiday

was a girl is ....

....

To my grandmother, the best thing about .... is ....

holiday

....

Molly's Christmas holiday was different during World War Two. Sugar and butter were scarce, so there were fewer cookies and treats. Most factories had to make war materials rather than new toys or Christmas tree ornaments. And Dad was far away in England helping wounded soldiers, so the family couldn't be together. But one thing didn't change—the hope for peace on earth.

My Grandmother's Holiday Story

As a girl, my father's mother celebrated ....
holiday

on .... My grandmother's favorite holiday
date

food was ....

Her family also ate ....

They decorated with ....

My grandmother thought the most beautiful decoration was ....

Today, that decoration is ....

Grandmother's favorite holiday clothes were ....

Her favorite tradition was ....

Something she did that is still a family tradition is ....

....

Presents (were / were not) a big part of holiday celebrations when my grandmother was a
circle one

girl because ....

A story my grandmother tells about .... when my father
holiday

was a boy is ....

....

To my grandmother, the best thing about .... is ....
holiday

Like many newly freed people during the Civil War, Addy and Momma didn't have the time or the money to put on much of a Christmas celebration at home. Church was the focus of their Christmas. They followed Reverend Drake's advice and gave what time and money they could spare to the Freedmen's Fund. They hoped their money might bring enslaved people like Poppa, Sam, and Esther to freedom someday.

My Birthday Story

I turned .... years old on .... To celebrate
date

my birthday, I ....

....

I had my birthday party at ....

People who came were ....

....

Things we did were ....

....

My favorite party game is ....

....

For decorations, we ....

....

My cake was ....

We also ate ....

I wore ....

A funny thing that happened was ....

....

Birthday gifts I received were ....

*F*elicity's tenth birthday party was a family affair. Mother decorated the parlor for a birthday breakfast, and Rose made fancy fruit tarts and a cake. Presents were not a big part of birthday parties in 1774, but a girl might receive a small gift such as a thimble. Mother made Felicity a pretty pompon of spring flowers to wear in her hair, and Grandfather gave her a new red silk ribbon for her guitar.

My favorite gift was .... from ....

Everyone went home with ....

....

The best thing about that birthday was ....

....

Now that I am older, ...

....

When I was born, my mother remembers ....

....

....

That day, my mother was .... years old, her mother was .... years old, and my father's

mother was .... years old. The best thing about being my age is ....

....

I would like to be .... years old, because ....

....

My birthday (is/is not) a good time of year for a birthday because ....
circle one

....

On my next birthday, I would like to ....

....

*F or her tenth birthday, Molly wanted an English tea party. England was America's **ally**, or partner, in the war. Emily, who knew all about the English princesses, helped Molly plan a party with a princess theme. The girls sent out elegant invitations and made paper crowns for party hats. Even their menu was an English and American partnership—tea and chocolate cake!*

My Mother's Birthday Story

My mother turned .... years old on .... To celebrate, date

she ....

When my mother was a girl, her birthday parties were like parties

today because ....

....

Birthday parties were different then because ....

....

My mother remembers a special party she had for her .... birthday. The party was special which one

because ....

....

Some of the guests were ....

The party took place at ....

For decorations, there were ....

Everyone played ....

They ate .... The birthday cake was ....

My mother wore ....

Some gifts she received were ....

When the party was over, everyone went home with ....

*Proper young ladies like Samantha had formal birthday parties in 1904. They wore their fanciest dresses and used their most ladylike manners. They talked politely and sometimes played quietly with dolls. At her tenth birthday party, Samantha served ten dainty little cakes called **petit fours**, and peppermint ice cream molded into fancy shapes. Too bad pesky Eddie Ryland ruined the ice cream!*

My mother's favorite birthday gift that she got as a girl was ....

She got it from .... when she was .... years old.

When she was my age, my mother looked forward to turning .... because ....
                                                                                              how old

....

She remembers feeling grown-up on her .... birthday because ....
                                                         which one

....

Her happiest birthday was her .... because ....
                                          which one

....

The most disappointing birthday my mother remembers was her .... birthday because
                                                                                              which one

....

The day my mother was born, her mother remembers ....

....

When my mother was my age, her mother was .... years old. Her mother's mother was

.... years old. My mother thinks the best thing about being my age was ....

....

She thinks the best thing about being her age right now is ....

....

She is looking forward to being .... because ....
                                              how old

....

In slavery, Addy's parents couldn't read or write, so nobody knew exactly what Addy's birth date was. This was true for many slaves and former slaves. So Addy decided to follow M'dear's advice and choose a special day to claim for her birthday. Addy chose a birthday that nobody in her family would ever forget!

My Grandmother's Birthday Story

My mother's mother turned .... years old on ....
date

When my grandmother was a girl, her birthday parties were like parties today

because ....

Birthday parties were different then because ....

....

For her .... birthday, my grandmother had a special birthday party. It was held
which one

at .... The decorations were ....
where

Everyone played ....

The birthday cake was .... They also ate ....

My grandmother wore ....

The happiest birthday my grandmother remembers was her .... because ....
which one

....

My grandmother says the best thing about being my age was ....

....

She thinks the best thing about being her age right now is ....

....

She would like to be .... because ....
how old

In 1824, families in New Mexico named each child after a Catholic saint, who was considered the child's special protector. Children didn't celebrate birthdays, but they did celebrate their saint's feast day each year. The saint's statue at the family altar was decorated with flowers, and family and friends gathered to enjoy music, treats, and a few simple gifts. Like many children, Josefina was named for the saint on whose day she was born— Saint Joseph—so her saint's day was her birthday!

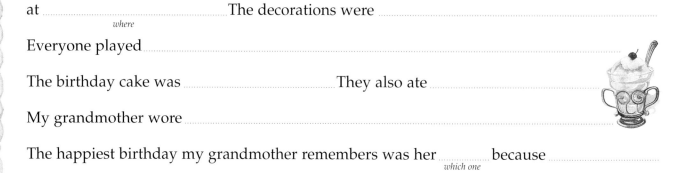

My Grandmother's Birthday Story

My father's mother turned .... years old on ....
date

When my grandmother was a girl, her birthday parties were like parties today

because ....

Birthday parties were different then because ....

....

For her .... birthday, my grandmother had a special birthday party. The party was held
which one

at .... The decorations were ....
where

Everyone played ....

The birthday cake was .... They also ate ....

My grandmother wore ....

The happiest birthday my grandmother remembers was her .... because ....
which one

....

My grandmother says the best thing about being my age was ....

....

She thinks the best thing about being her age right now is ....

....

She would like to be .... because ....
how old

....

Kirsten didn't expect a party for her tenth birthday. Pioneers had lots of work and little time for play. But frontier families often made their work fun by doing it together. The Larsons' barn-raising party was the day before Kirsten's birthday, so it became a special birthday celebration. Kirsten was even more surprised when her friends gave her the friendship quilt as a birthday present!

My Vacation Story

School ends on ....
date

During the summer, I like to ....

The best thing to do on a summer afternoon is ....

....

On summer days I sometimes go to ....

....

My favorite summer clothes are ....

My family celebrates the Fourth of July by ....

In the summer I take a vacation to ....

I go for .... I go with ....
how long   *names of people you go with*

On my vacation this year ....
Tell about what you did or what happened.

....

....

On our vacations, my family often travels by ....
car, airplane, bus, train, boat

The farthest we ever traveled was ...., when we went to ....
distance   *where*

To pass the time, we ....
Tell about games you play or songs you sing.

....

The most fun I had on vacation was

The worst time was

I will never forget the time

I wish I could forget

My souvenirs include

One of my favorite outdoor games is

To play,

Explain how game is played.

For Samantha, camping with Grandmary at Piney Point wasn't like camping today! In 1904, camps were comfortable summer homes in the woods or mountains. Servants did all the work. Girls like Samantha had fun swimming, boating, picnicking, and painting. Samantha also made her own souvenirs—she pressed wildflowers and sewed a tiny pillow filled with spicy pine needles.

What I like best about summer vacation is

Someday, I would like to take a vacation to

because

My Mother's Vacation Story

During the summer, my mother likes to ....

....

When she was a girl, in the summer she would sometimes go to ....

....

Her favorite summer clothes were ....

My mother celebrated the Fourth of July by ....

....

When she was .... years old, my mother took a vacation to ....

.... She was gone ....
how long

She went with ....
names of people she went with

....

When they took vacations, her family usually traveled by ....
car, aiplane, bus, train, boat

The farthest they ever traveled was ...., when they went to ....
distance

....

To pass the time, they ....
Tell about games your mother played or songs she sang.

....

When my mother was a girl, one of her favorite outdoor games was ....

....

Kirsten couldn't wait for the Fourth of July. It was her whole summer vacation! After morning chores, the Larsons went to town for the parade. But they had to return in time for evening chores. Today, people sometimes do pioneer work on their summer vacations! Kirsten's favorite jobs were fishing and hunting in the woods for wild berries. Nowadays vacationers go fishing and hiking in the woods just for fun.

To play, ...

Explain how game is played.

....

After my parents were married, they took a vacation to ....

....

The best vacation my mother remembers was when she went to ....

.... She went with ....

....

A story she tells about that vacation is ....

....

....

The worst vacation my mother ever took was to ....

when she was .... years old. On that vacation ....

....

....

The thing my mother likes best about summer vacations is ....

....

....

Someday, my mother would like to take a vacation to ....

because ....

Addy's family couldn't afford to take a summer vacation in 1865, but Addy looked forward to a day of fun at the church fair. There would be pony rides, games, and barbecued chicken. And best of all, the fair was for a good cause—the money it raised would go to help people who were separated from their families or wounded during the Civil War.

My Grandmother's Vacation Story

During the summer, my mother's mother likes to ....

....

When she was a girl, my grandmother would sometimes have her

summer vacation at ....

Her favorite summer clothes were ....

My grandmother celebrated the Fourth of July by..

When she was .... years old, my grandmother took a vacation to ....

She went with ....

names of people she went with

She was gone .... Her family usually traveled by ....

how long   *car, airplane, bus, train, boat*

To pass the time, they ....

Tell about games your grandmother played or songs she sang.

When she was a girl, one of Grandmother's favorite outdoor games was ....

.... To play, ...

Explain how game is played.

....

After my grandparents were married, they took a vacation to ....

The best vacation my grandmother remembers was when she went to ....

with .... A story she tells about that vacation is ....

....

Someday my grandmother would like to visit ....

In 1774, roads were poor, and travel—by horse and carriage—was slow. So people rarely went on trips or took vacations. When they did, they often stayed a long time. Felicity spent the entire summer at Grandfather's plantation, riding Penny and playing lazily by the river. The peaceful plantation was only six miles from busy, bustling Williamsburg, but it seemed like another world.

My Grandmother's Vacation Story

During the summer, my father's mother likes to ....

....

When she was a girl, my grandmother would sometimes have a summer

vacation at ....

Her favorite summer clothes were ....

My grandmother celebrated the Fourth of July by ....

When she was .... years old, my grandmother took a vacation to ....

She went with ....
.... *names of people she went with*

She was gone .... Her family usually traveled by ....
.... *how long* .... *car, airplane, bus, train, boat*

To pass the time, they ....
.... *Tell about games your grandmother played or songs she sang.*

When she was a girl, one of Grandmother's favorite outdoor games was ....

.... To play, ...
.... *Explain how game is played.*

....

After my grandparents were married, they took a vacation to ....

The best vacation my grandmother remembers was when she went to ....

with .... A story she tells about that vacation is ....

....

....

Someday my grandmother would like to visit ....

*T*he daily work of farming made it hard for families like the Montoyas to leave home. But Josefina got to go along on short trips, like a visit to the Indian pueblo or to her grandparents' home in Santa Fe. Although these were often business trips for Papá, they were like vacations for Josefina. She could spend an afternoon playing dolls by the stream with her Pueblo friend Mariana or taking in the sights of the huge marketplace in Santa Fe.

*F*elicity found running and riding horses much easier in Ben's breeches—but she couldn't let anyone see her wearing them! In 1774, girls and women always wore long dresses and tight stays. They were not supposed to get dirty or sweaty or out of breath. But Felicity grew impatient with quiet, fussy activities like sewing and serving tea. Today, girls can wear what they like—and do what they like.

Changes for Me

The best thing about me right now is ....

....

....

I would like to change so that ....

....

I *never* want .... to change, because ....

....

Today, it is fashionable to wear ....

It is unfashionable to ....
List unfashionable things to do and wear.

I will *never* wear ....

Popular toys today are ....

My favorite game or activity is ....

My favorite music is ....

I listen to it on ....
radio, tapes, CDs, television

My mother thinks it sounds ....

I like to read ....
favorite books and magazines

My favorite television programs are ....

My favorite movies are ....

Today it costs about .... to go to the movies. I get spending money by ....

.... I usually have about .... of my own.
how much money

I like to buy ....

These are things that cost 1¢ .... 10¢ ....

50¢ .... $1 ....

$5 .... $25 ....

Something I'd like that's too expensive is .... It costs ....

I am saving up to buy ....

I like to say .... when I mean ....

and .... when I mean ....

A new invention today is ....

An important change happening in the world today is ....

....

I think this change is (good/not good) because ....
circle one

....

I hope the world will change so that ....

....

The best thing about being an American girl today is ....

*A*fter she moved to New York City with Uncle Gard and Aunt Cornelia, Samantha got an important letter from Nellie. The letter might have been sent through a pneumatic (new-MAT-ik) tube—a system like the tubes we use today at drive-up banks. Miles of underground tubes carried the mail under the city's streets from post office to post office. Then it was delivered to homes by horse-drawn wagon—and, starting in 1906, by motorcar.

Changes for My Mother

When my mother was a girl, it was fashionable to wear ....

.... It was

unfashionable to .... My mother thought

Name an unfashionable thing to do or wear.

she would *never* wear .... Popular toys when my mother was

growing up were ....

My mother liked to play ....

favorite games

Her favorite music was ....

She listened to it on .... Her mother thought it

radio, records, tapes, CDs, television

sounded .... I think it sounds ....

When my mother was my age, her favorite books were ....

....

Her favorite television programs were ....

Her favorite movies were ....

When my mother was my age, it cost .... to go to the movies. My mother got spending

money by .... She usually had about .... of her own.

how much

These are things that cost 1¢ .... 10¢ ....

50¢ .... $1 ....

$5 .... $25 ....

Something she wanted that was too expensive was

It cost .... My mother saved up her money to buy

When she was a girl, my mother liked to say

when she meant .... and

.... when she meant

A new invention was

An important change happening in the world was

When my mother was my age, the world was different for girls because

She thought that by the year 2000

One of the biggest changes in my mother's life has been

She never thought that she would see

Today, she hopes

*I*n Kirsten's day, babies
were born at home. On the
frontier there were no doctors
or hospitals nearby, so neigh-
bors, relatives, or women
called midwives helped at
births. Pioneer families often
had lots of children, so they
could help with all the farm
chores. But many children
died of sicknesses like influenza
and cholera, as Marta did.
Today, modern hospitals and
medicines help most children
live to adulthood.

Changes for My Grandmother

When my mother's mother was a girl, it was fashionable to wear

....

It was unfashionable to ....
Name an unfashionable thing to do or wear.

My grandmother thought she would *never* wear ....

Popular toys when my grandmother was growing up were ....

My grandmother liked to play ....
favorite games

Her favorite music was ....

She listened to it on .... Her mother thought it sounded ....
radio or records

I think it sounds .... When my grandmother was my age,

her favorite book was ....

Her favorite movie was ....

It cost .... to go to the movies. My grandmother went ....
how often

My grandmother got spending money by ....

.... She usually had about .... of her own.
how much

These are things that cost 1¢ ....

5¢ .... 10¢ ....

50¢ .... $1 ....

$5 .... $25 ....

*T*he Civil War brightened the future for Addy and other African Americans. Addy could continue her education and perhaps go to college. New laws gave citizenship and voting rights to former slaves. But life in freedom was not easy. Many white people treated black people poorly and wouldn't hire them or sell them anything. Changes happened slowly—and they are still happening today.

Something my grandmother wanted that was too expensive was ....

It cost .... My grandmother saved up her money to buy ....

When she was a girl, my grandmother liked to say ....

when she meant .... and ....

.... when she meant ....

A new invention was ....

An important change happening in the world was ....

....

When my grandmother was my age, things were different for girls because ....

....

She thought that by the year 2000 ....

....

The biggest change in my grandmother's life has been ....

....

She never thought that she would see ....

....

....

Today, she hopes ....

....

Samantha's friend Nellie earned $1.80 a week working in a thread factory. Children who worked in factories had no time for school or play. They worked 12 hours a day, every day but Sunday. They had to stand all day by large, dangerous machines, sometimes climbing up on them to fix them. Today there are laws against young children working—and safety laws for all factory workers.

Changes for My Grandmother

When my father's mother was a girl, it was fashionable to

wear ....

Josefina and her family spoke Spanish, because their ancestors had come from Spain. They also heard Indian languages spoken by the Pueblo people who lived nearby. When traders from America came to New Mexico, they brought not only new goods and ideas— they brought new languages, like English, French, and German. Today in the United States there are still many languages spoken—more than one hundred in some big cities!

It was unfashionable to ....
Name an unfashionable thing to do or wear.

My grandmother thought she would *never* wear ....

Popular toys when my grandmother was growing up were ......

My grandmother liked to play ....
favorite games

Her favorite music was ....

She listened to it on .... Her mother thought it sounded ....
radio or records

I think it sounds................................... When my grandmother was my age,

her favorite book was ....

Her favorite movie was ....

It cost.............. to go to the movies. My grandmother went ....
how often

My grandmother got spending money by ....

.... She usually had about .... of her own.
how much

These are things that cost 1¢ ....

5¢ .... 10¢ ....

50¢ .... $1 ....

$5 .... $25 ....

Something my grandmother wanted that was too expensive was ....

It cost .... My grandmother saved up her money to buy ....

When she was a girl, my grandmother liked to say ....

when she meant .... and ....

.... when she meant ....

A new invention was ....

An important change happening in the world was ....

....

When my grandmother was my age, things were different for girls because ....

....

She thought that by the year 2000 ....

....

The biggest change in my grandmother's life has been ....

....

She never thought that she would see ....

....

Today, she hopes ....

When Felicity was a girl, people could be put in prison for their beliefs. Elizabeth's father was jailed for being a Loyalist, a colonist who was loyal to the king of England. After the Revolutionary War, the new government of the United States of America decided that people should be able to believe what they wanted—and say what they believed. Our Bill of Rights still protects these freedoms.

Photographs

THE AMERICAN GIRLS COLLECTION®

FELICITY · JOSEFINA · KIRSTEN · ADDY · SAMANTHA · MOLLY

The American Girls Collection tells the stories of six lively girls who lived long ago—Felicity, Josefina, Kirsten, Addy, Samantha, and Molly. As you read about their adventures, you'll learn what growing up was like in times past.

And while this series of beautifully illustrated books of historical fiction is the heart of The American Girls Collection, it is only the beginning. Our lovable dolls and their beautiful clothes and accessories make the stories in The American Girls Collection come alive.

The American Girls Collection is for you if you love to curl up with a good book. It's for you if you like to play with dolls and act out stories. It's for you if you want to collect something so special that you will treasure it for years to come.

To learn more about The American Girls Collection, send us the postcard below, or call **1-800-845-0005**. We'll send you a catalogue full of books, dolls, dresses, and other delights for girls. You can also visit our Web site at **www.americangirl.com**.

Detach card at perforated lines.

I'm an American girl who loves to get mail. Please send me a catalogue of The American Girls Collection®:

My name is _____

My address is _____

City _____

My birth date is ___ Mo

Parent's signature

Due to a printing error, this card does not meet postal regulations.

To receive your FREE American Girl™ catalogue, please call 1-800-845-0005.

Zip _____

1961

And send a catalogue to my friend:

My friend's name is _____

Address _____

City _____ State _____ Zip _____

1225

If the postcard has already
been removed from this book
and you would like to receive
an American Girl® catalogue,
please send your name and
address to:

AMERICAN GIRL
PO BOX 620497
MIDDLETON WI 53562-9940

Or call our toll-free number:
1-800-845-0005